WHERE DOES CHRISTMAS COME FROM?

Children's Holidays & Celebrations Books

Speedy Publishing LLC
40 E. Main St. #1156
Newark, DE 19711
www.speedypublishing.com

Christmas is both a holy religious occasion and an overall cultural and commercial phenomenon.

Christmas is the date put aside for the celebration of the birth of Jesus Christ.

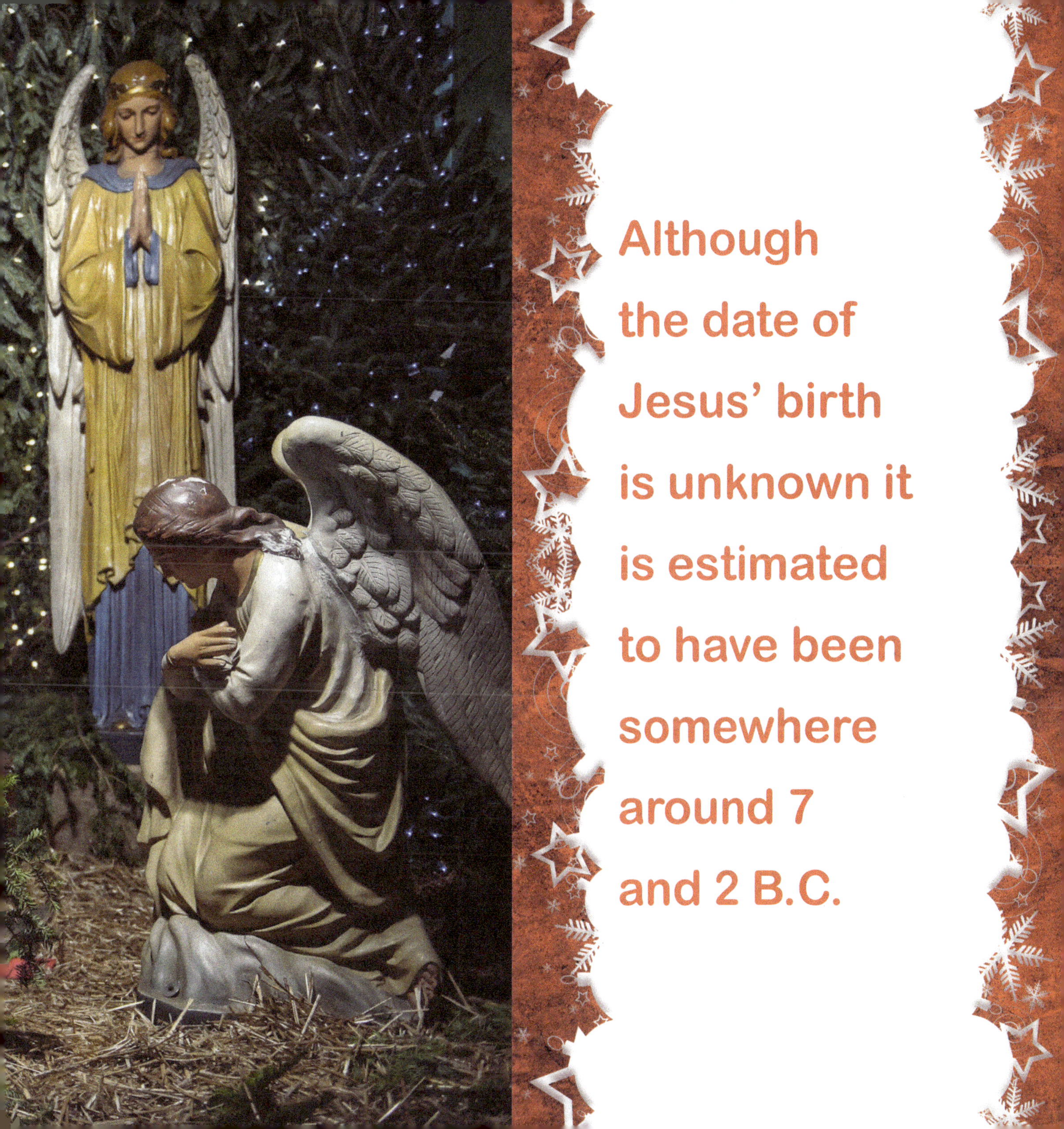

Although the date of Jesus' birth is unknown it is estimated to have been somewhere around 7 and 2 B.C.

The three wise men who visited Mary and Joseph when Jesus was born brought gold, frankincense and myrrh as gifts.

Christians
celebrate
it on
December 25
everywhere
throughout
the world.

Christians observe Christmas Day as the anniversary of the birth of Jesus in Nazareth.

Christmas
really
originates
from "Mass
of Christ".

People from around the world have been observing the tradition for more than 2000 years.

Merry Christmas

Popular traditions include exchanging gifts, attending church, decorating Christmas trees and waiting for Santa Claus to arrive.

X implies Christ in Greek so we sometimes use the word X-Mas as an abbreviation for the word Christmas.

A typical figure known all through the world and connected with Christmas is Santa Claus.

All the gifts in the Twelve Days of Christmas song would equal to 364 gifts.

Christmas lights were invented in 1882 by Edward Johnson.

Christmas trees were first decorated with foods such as apples and nuts.

The tradition of Christmas caroling started as an early English custom.

St. Francis of Assisi started the custom of singing Christmas tunes in chapel in the thirteenth century.

Children often perform in nativity plays at Christmas.

We can truly be happy during Christmas season!

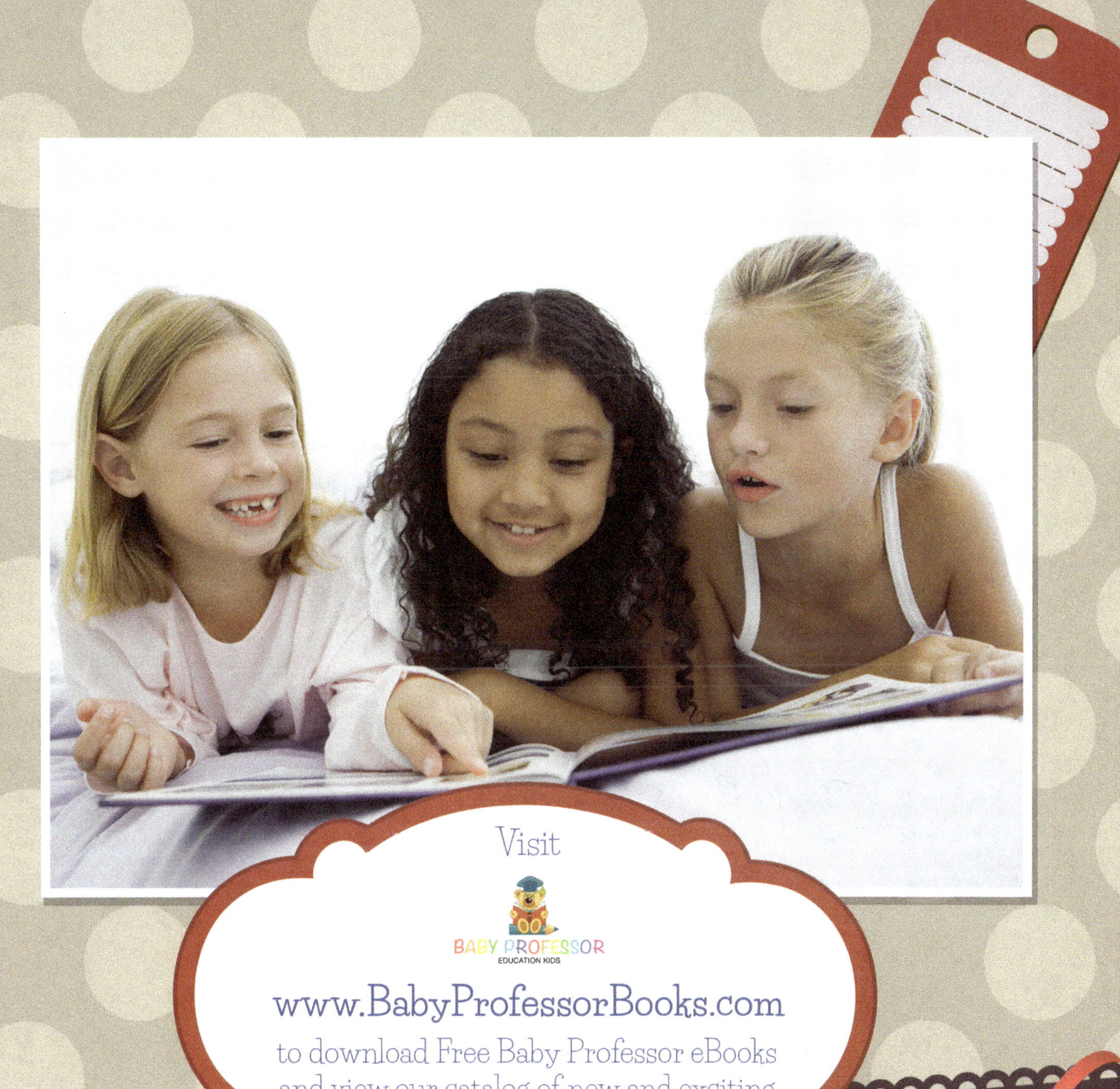
Visit
BABY PROFESSOR
EDUCATION KIDS
www.BabyProfessorBooks.com
to download Free Baby Professor eBooks
and view our catalog of new and exciting
Children's Books

www.ingramcontent.com/pod-product-compliance
Lightning Source LLC
LaVergne TN
LVHW060832170826
845678LV00010B/1960

* 9 7 9 8 8 6 9 4 4 4 2 9 5 *